SCHOLASTIC

READ & RESPOND

Bringing the best books to life in the classroom

Activities based on George's Marvellous Medicine
By Roald Dahl

Terms and conditions

IMPORTANT – PERMITTED USE AND WARNINGS – READ CAREFULLY BEFORE USING

IF YOU ACCEPT THE ABOVE CONDITIONS YOU MAY PROCEED TO USE THE CD-ROM.

Recommended system requirements:
Windows: XP (Service Pack 3), Vista (Service Pack 2), Windows 7 or Windows 8 with 2.33GHz processor
Mac: OS 10.6 to 10.8 with Intel Core™ Duo processor
1GB RAM (recommended)
1024 x 768 Screen resolution
CD-ROM drive (24x speed recommended)
Adobe Reader (version 9 recommended for Mac users)
Broadband internet connections (for installation and updates)

For all technical support queries (including no CD drive), please phone Scholastic Customer Services on 0845 6039091.

Designed using Adobe Indesign
Scholastic Education, an imprint of Scholastic Ltd
Book End, Range Road, Witney, Oxfordshire, OX29 0YD
Registered office: Westfield Road, Southam, Warwickshire CV47 0RA

Printed and bound by Ashford Colour Press
© 2016 Scholastic Ltd
2 3 4 5 6 7 8 9   6 7 8 9 0 1 2 3 4 5
British Library Cataloguing-in-Publication Data
A catalogue record for this book is available from the British Library.
ISBN 978-1407-16061-0

Due to the nature of the web, we cannot guarantee the content or links of any site mentioned. We strongly recommend that teachers check websites before using them in the classroom.

Author Eileen Jones
Editorial team Rachel Morgan, Jenny Wilcox, Kate Pedlar, Rebecca Rothwell
Series designer Neil Salt
Designer Anna Oliwa
Illustrator Kate Sheppard/Beehive Illustration
Digital development Hannah Barnett, Phil Crothers and MWA Technologies Private Ltd

Acknowledgements
The publishers gratefully acknowledge permission to reproduce the following copyright material:
David Higham for the use of the text from *George's Marvellous Medicine* written by Roald Dahl, illustated by Quentin Blake. © 1981, Roald Dahl Nominee Ltd (1981, Jonathan Cape Ltd).
A P Watt at United Agents on behalf of Quentin Blake for permission to use the illustration from *George's Marvellous Medicine*.
Penguin Books Ltd UK for the use of the cover from *George's Marvellous Medicine* written by Roald Dahl, illustrated by Quentin Blake (Puffin, 2016).

Every effort has been made to trace copyright holders for the works reproduced in this book, and the publishers apologise for any inadvertent omissions.

CONTENTS ▼

Introduction   4

Using the CD-ROM   5

Curriculum links   6

About the book and author   8

Guided reading   9

Shared reading   13

Grammar, punctuation & spelling   19

Plot, character & setting   25

Talk about it   32

Get writing   38

Assessment   44

INTRODUCTION

Read & Respond provides teaching ideas related to a specific children's book. The series focuses on best-loved books and brings you ways to use them to engage your class and enthuse them about reading.

The book is divided into different sections:

- **About the book and author:** gives you some background information about the book and the author.

- **Guided reading:** breaks the book down into sections and gives notes for using it with guided reading groups. A bookmark has been provided on page 12 containing comprehension questions. The children can be directed to refer to these as they read.

- **Shared reading:** provides extracts from the children's books with associated notes for focused work. There is also one non-fiction extract that relates to the children's book.

- **Grammar, punctuation & spelling:** provides word-level work related to the children's book so you can teach grammar, punctuation and spelling in context.

- **Plot, character & setting:** contains activity ideas focused on the plot, characters and the setting of the story.

- **Talk about it:** has speaking and listening activities related to the children's book. These activities may be based directly on the children's book or be broadly based on the themes and concepts of the story.

- **Get writing:** provides writing activities related to the children's book. These activities may be based directly on the children's book or be broadly based on the themes and concepts of the story.

- **Assessment:** contains short activities that will help you assess whether the children have understood concepts and curriculum objectives. They are designed to be informal activities to feed into your planning.

The activities follow the same format:

- **Objective:** the objective for the lesson. It will be based upon a curriculum objective, but will often be more specific to the focus being covered.

- **What you need:** a list of resources you need to teach the lesson, including digital resources (printable pages, interactive activities and media resources, see page 5).

- **What to do:** the activity notes.

- **Differentiation:** this is provided where specific and useful differentiation advice can be given to support and/or extend the learning in the activity. Differentiation by providing additional adult support has not been included as this will be at a teacher's discretion based upon specific children's needs and ability, as well as the availability of support.

The activities are numbered for reference within each section and should move through the text sequentially – so you can use the lesson while you are reading the book. Once you have read the book, most of the activities can be used in any order you wish.

Below are brief guidance notes for using the CD-ROM. For more detailed information, please click on the '?' button in the top right-hand corner of the screen.

The program contains the following:
- the extract pages from the book
- all of the photocopiable pages from the book
- additional printable pages
- interactive on-screen activities
- media resources.

Getting started

Put the CD-ROM into your CD-ROM drive. If you do not have a CD-ROM drive, phone Scholastic Customer Services on 0845 6039091.

- For Windows users, the install wizard should autorun, if it fails to do so then navigate to your CD-ROM drive. Then follow the installation process.
- For Mac users, copy the disk image file to your hard drive. After it has finished copying double click it to mount the disk image. Navigate to the mounted disk image and run the installer. After installation the disk image can be unmounted and the DMG can be deleted from the hard drive.
- To install on a network, see the ReadMe file located on the CD-ROM (navigate to your drive).

To complete the installation of the program you need to open the program and click 'Update' in the pop-up. Please note – this CD-ROM is web-enabled and the content will be downloaded from the internet to your hard drive to populate the CD-ROM with the relevant resources. This only needs to be done on first use, after this you will be able to use the CD-ROM without an internet connection. If at any point any content is updated, you will receive another pop-up upon start up when there is an internet connection.

Main menu

The main menu is the first screen that appears. Here you can access: terms and conditions, registration links, how to use the CD-ROM and credits. To access a specific book click on the relevant button (NB only titles installed will be available). You can filter by the

drop-down lists if you wish. You can search all resources by clicking 'Search' in the bottom left-hand corner. You can also log in and access favourites that you have bookmarked.

Resources

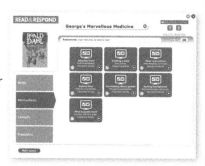

By clicking on a book on the Main menu, you are taken to the resources for that title. The resources are: Media, Interactives, Extracts and Printables. Select the category and then launch a resource by clicking the play button.

Teacher settings

In the top right-hand corner of the screen is a small 'T' icon. This is the teacher settings area. It is password protected, the password is: login. This area will allow you to choose the print quality settings for interactive activities ('Default' or 'Best') and also allow you to check for updates to the program or re-download all content to the disk via Refresh all content. You can also set up user logins so that you can save and access favourites. Once a user is set up, they can enter by clicking the login link underneath the 'T' and '?' buttons.

Search

You can access an all resources search by clicking the search button on the bottom left of the Main menu. You can search for activities by type (using the drop-down filter) or by keyword by typing into the box. You can then assign resources to your favourites area or launch them directly from the search area.

CURRICULUM LINKS

Section	Activity	Curriculum objectives
Guided reading		Comprehension: To ask questions to improve their understanding of the text.
Shared reading	1	Comprehension: To identify how language contributes to meaning.
	2	Comprehension: To draw inferences such as inferring characters' feelings, thoughts and motives from their actions, and justifying inferences with evidence.
	3	Comprehension: To identify how language contributes to meaning; to draw inferences such as inferring characters' feelings, thoughts and motives from their actions, and justifying inferences with evidence.
	4	Comprehension: To read books that are structured in different ways and to read for different purposes.
Grammar, punctuation & spelling	1	Transcription: To use further prefixes and understand how to add them.
	2	Composition: To use fronted adverbials.
	3	Composition: To extend the range of sentences with more than one clause by using a wider range of conjunctions.
	4	Transcription: To spell further homophones.
	5	Composition: To use and punctuate direct speech.
	6	Composition: To indicate possession by using the possessive apostrophe with plural nouns.
Plot, character & setting	1	Comprehension: To predict what might happen from details stated and implied.
	2	Comprehension: To prepare poems to read aloud and perform them.
	3	Comprehension: To draw inferences and justify inferences with evidence.
	4	Comprehension: To discuss words and phrases that capture the reader's interest and imagination.
	5	Comprehension: To identify themes and conventions in a wide range of books.
	6	Comprehension: To infer characters' feelings and motives from their actions.
	7	Comprehension: To read books that are structured in different ways.
	8	Comprehension: To ask questions to improve their understanding of the text.

Section	Activity	Curriculum objectives
Talk about it	1	Spoken language: To use spoken language to develop understanding through speculating, hypothesising, imagining and exploring ideas.
	2	Spoken language: To participate in role play. Comprehension: To infer characters' feelings and motives from their actions.
	3	Spoken language: To give well-structured narratives for different purposes, including for expressing feelings.
	4	Spoken language: To participate in discussions and debates.
	5	Spoken language: To select and use appropriate registers for effective communication.
	6	Spoken language: To use spoken language to develop understanding through speculating, hypothesising, imagining and exploring ideas.
Get writing	1	Composition: To discuss writing similar to that which they are planning to write in order to understand and learn from its structure, vocabulary and grammar.
	2	Composition: To choose pronouns appropriately for clarity and cohesion and to avoid repetition.
	3	Composition: To draft and write, organising paragraphs around a theme.
	4	Composition: To plan their writing by discussing and recording ideas.
	5	Composition: To draft a narrative, creating settings, characters and plot.
	6	Composition: To compose and rehearse sentences orally.
Assessment	1	Composition: To indicate possession by using the possessive apostrophe with plural nouns; to punctuate direct speech; to extend the range of sentences by using a variety of conjunctions.
	2	Comprehension: To discuss words and phrases that capture the reader's interest and imagination.
	3	Composition: To discuss writing similar to that which they are planning to write in order to understand and learn from its structure, vocabulary and grammar; to draft and write non-narrative material, using simple organisational devices.
	4	Comprehension: To identify themes and conventions in a wide range of books.
	5	Spoken language: To give well-structured narratives for different purposes, including for expressing feelings.
	6	Composition: To draft a narrative, creating settings, characters and plot.

GEORGE'S MARVELLOUS MEDICINE

About the book

George's Marvellous Medicine is an ideal book for Key Stage 2 study. Exciting, inventive and funny, it is an exhilarating read by a famous children's author, and has been adapted for the stage.

The main character is George Kranky, a lonely and bored eight-year-old boy, who lives on an isolated farm. When George is left to look after his cantankerous grandma one Saturday morning, he finds the prospect dull. With George's parents out of the way, she delights in tormenting George, grumbling that he should stop growing by eating cabbage with boiled caterpillars, taunting him with threats of her magic powers, and frightening him so that he shuts himself in a different room. It is then that George makes his plan: he will substitute her usual medicine with a homemade one that will make her less horrid. In a race against the medication deadline of 11 o'clock, George makes a medicine with startling effects. Grandma becomes gigantic! George's father, rather than being angry or upset when he returns to a broken house with Grandma sticking through the roof, is excited about the business prospects of enormous animals. Once the impulsive Mr Kranky is involved, matters get out of hand. Mr Kranky's ambitions require more of George's medicine, but versions two, three and four fail to achieve the positive results of George's original mixture. The animals become oddities that no customers will want. As for Grandma, her fate is so shocking that George wonders if he is the one with magic powers.

About the author

Roald Dahl was born of Norwegian parents in Llandaff, South Wales in 1916. He attended Llandaff Cathedral School and Repton School, but he was not a happy pupil. Keen to travel to magical faraway places, he worked for Shell, the large oil company, when he left school. He was sent to East Africa, but he hated the snakes! A variety of other jobs followed: RAF fighter pilot in the Second World War, air attaché and author.

Roald Dahl's early writing was for adults. However, it was later, as a writer of children's books, that Roald Dahl achieved greatest success. Claiming to 'know what children like', he demonstrated a fantastic ability to look at life from a child's point of view; he believed children's writers have to get down on their hands and knees and look up at the adults towering over them, telling them what to do. His extensive output included *James and the Giant Peach*, *Fantastic Mr Fox*, *Charlie and the Chocolate Factory*, *The Enormous Crocodile* and *Matilda* (voted the most popular children's book on World Book Day in 1999), and many more. Roald Dahl died in 1990.

Key facts

George's Marvellous Medicine

Author: Roald Dahl

Illustrator: Quentin Blake

First published: 1981 by Jonathan Cape

Did you know: Roald Dahl wrote many of his books in a white hut at the bottom of his garden. The hut was built from bricks and had a yellow front door – yellow was his favourite colour.

The cover and the first chapter – Grandma

Direct the children to the cover. Ask: *Who is the author? Why is there another name?* (Quentin Blake is the illustrator.) How do the children respond to the cover? Do the title and illustrations make them want to read the book?

Read the preliminary 'Warning to Readers' and the opening chapter. Talk about the chapter's function: to hook the reader. Discuss important 'W' questions. (Who? What? Why? Where? When?) Have some been answered? Point out: character introductions; the subjects of boredom, loneliness and unease ('Could it be, George wondered, that she was a witch?'); an isolated farm location; a boring Saturday morning. Assess the chapter's success. Is the reader hooked by the immediate introduction of the title character and a worrying situation?

The Marvellous Plan

Point out the italicised words in the first paragraph. Ask: *What two feelings do they describe?* (They suggest an intense dislike of Grandma and an urge to do something astounding about her.) Comment that George is only young: he is frightened by Grandma, but fears actually hurting her. Read out 'he wanted suddenly to explode her away. Well…not quite away.' Examine Blake's illustrations. Ask: *How has he decided what to draw?* (The pictures follow Dahl's words.) Comment on the chapter's title. Ask: *Why is it appropriate?* (All George does is plan.) *What does he decide?* ('A magic medicine it shall be!') Compare this illustration's gleeful expression with the illustrations earlier in the chapter showing George looking puzzled. Read George's plan aloud. Ask: *What format is used?* (It's in rhyming couplets.) *Is the tone serious or light-hearted?* Ask the children to discuss question 1 on the Guided Reading bookmark (page 12).

George Begins to Make the Medicine

Investigate George's choice of medicine contents. What is his rule? ('…if it was runny, or powdery or gooey, in it went.') Point out the capital letters for products and their details. Ask: *Is this writing device effective? What is emphasised?* (the unsuitability of the ingredients) Comment on the fast pace as George moves to different places, finding ingredients. Direct the children to the reference to 11 o'clock on the first page of the book. Suggest that George's hurried actions emphasise his limited time. Ask: *How else does Roald Dahl remind the reader of a time limit?* (the dialogue at the end of the chapter) Encourage discussion of questions 3 and 6 on the Guided Reading bookmark.

Animal Pills

Read the title of the chapter and discuss question 2 on the Guided Reading bookmark. Read aloud the chapter's first three paragraphs. Ask: *What do they reveal about George?* (He is obedient.) Discuss the humour in George's spoken commentary. Ask: *How is George being funny?* (He applies the pills' information to Grandma.) Point out examples: 'the old bird won't be losing any feathers'; 'grumpy old cow in the living-room'. Ask the children to discuss question 11 on the bookmark.

The Cook-up

Point out the passing of time: it is twenty to eleven. Suggest that this urgency could be why George has turned up the gas 'as high as it would go'. Investigate the evocative language in the long paragraph describing the cooking process. Ask: *Which senses does Roald Dahl appeal to?* (smell and sight) *What writing devices are used?* (alliteration, onomatopoeia, simile) Comment on the steam's effect on George. Ask: *What does Roald Dahl 'turn' George and the saucepan into?* (a witch and her cauldron) Read George's chant aloud. Ask: *Which alliterative sounds are noticeable? Is the vocabulary strange?* Ask partners to check the meaning of words in the chant, identifying made up words ('spissing'). Discuss question 7 on the Guided Reading bookmark.

Brown Paint

Comment on the brevity of this chapter and the previous one. Ask: *Why did Dahl not combine them?* (There is a change of focus and atmosphere.) Point out the reminder of the time deadline. Investigate the chapter's final seven paragraphs. Examine the excited short sentences and the urgent exclamation marks. Comment on Grandma's speech. Is Dahl making fun of his character by giving her these words? (She is looking forward to her usual medicine that improves her health; George's 'magic mixture' could have any effect on her.) Encourage discussion of question 8 on the Guided Reading bookmark.

Grandma Gets the Medicine

Before reading the chapter, use question 2 on the Guided Reading bookmark for partner and class discussion. Ask: *Is this likely to be a pivotal chapter?* (Events so far have been leading up to this point.) Read the chapter. Ask: *What is the effect of the medicine on Grandma compared to?* (an electric shock and a fire) Explore other physical details: changing colour, inflating and deflating, standing independently and growing. Consider the dialogue. How does George sound at first? (excited) What about Grandma? Suggest that she is puzzled and angry. Direct the children to the final five paragraphs. Ask: *How have the characters' reactions changed?* (Grandma now sounds excited; George is worried.) Discuss question 10 on the Guided Reading bookmark.

The Brown Hen

Point out Grandma's boast of 'magic powers' and 'wizardry in the tips of my fingers'. Remind the children of her talk of 'magic powers' in the first chapter. Ask: *What do Grandma and George argue about when her head comes through the roof?* (She thinks that she is responsible and dismisses George's talk of his new medicine.) *How does George prove his medicine's power?* (He gives some to the hen.) Investigate Grandma and George's conversation about the hen. Point out their shared excitement at the hen's growth. Read the final two paragraphs aloud. Ask: *Do George and Grandma actually seem friends?* Comment that the reader has not yet met George's father. Refer to George's worry about the roof at the end of the previous chapter, and Grandma's threat in this chapter of, 'Your father'll be after you now!' What type of person do the children expect? Ask the children to discuss question 5 on the Guided Reading bookmark.

The Pig, the Bullocks, the Sheep, the Pony and the Nanny-goat

Read the chapter and ask: *Is Mr Kranky what you expected?* Point out that he is 'a kind father to George'. Ask: *Why is he difficult to live with?* ('Even the smallest things got him all worked up and excited'.) Comment on his sharp speech and abrupt dismissal of Grandma. Ask: *What is he interested in?* (the giant hen) Point out the enthusiastic speed at which Mr Kranky rushes George and his medicine around the animals. Ask the children to study the illustrations. Do they contribute to their enjoyment of this chapter? Why? Ask: *Why do you think Mr Kranky is so pleased?* Direct the children to question 4 on the Guided Reading bookmark.

A Crane for Grandma

Before reading the chapter, use question 2 on the Guided Reading bookmark for partner and class discussion. Comment on Dahl's description of the four characters in paragraph one. What is strange about what is happening? (Grandma's predicament is being ignored.) Point out the contrast between the three Krankys' treatment of Grandma. Ask: *Why is Mrs Kranky more concerned than the others?* (Grandma is her mother.) *How has George's medicine changed Grandma for the better?* (Her aches and pain have gone, so her mood has improved.) Comment on the absurdity of this chapter. Do the children find it funny? Why? Direct the children to question 5 on the bookmark to discuss the contribution made by dialogue to the humour.

Mr Kranky's Great Idea

Before reading the chapter, use question 2 on the Guided Reading bookmark for partners to share ideas. Afterwards, share predictions. Look at the first page of the chapter and ask: *What is suggested by the exclamation mark?* (Mr Kranky's demand for speedy action) Compare his excited greed with George's caution ('But, wait a minute, Dad') and Mrs Kranky's complacency ('Do calm down, my dear'). Point out places later where Dahl's writing style of lists, jerky phrases and short sentences matches the characters' hurried movement. Read aloud the final paragraph. Ask: *Is Mr Kranky expecting too much?* Discuss question 12 on the Guided Reading bookmark.

Marvellous Medicine Number Two

Comment on the pressure Mr Kranky puts on George. Do the children think that this pressure may be causing George to forget things? Ask: *What does George say that reveals his doubts about this new medicine?* ('At least I hope it is.') *How does Dahl want the reader to react to the changed hen? Is it intended to be funny?* (Humorous illustrations may suggest this.) Comment that Mr Kranky is confident when he sets off for the village. Ask: *Why? Which words suggest that he is sure he has the solution?* ('No *wonder* it went wrong'.) Ask the children to discuss questions 9 and 11 on the Guided Reading bookmark.

Marvellous Medicine Number Three

Indicate the chapter title and comment that Dahl 'signposts' what will happen with clear titles such as this. Together discuss question 8 on the Guided Reading bookmark. Ask: *What doesn't this title reveal?* (whether or not the medicine will work) Comment on Mr Kranky's excited anticipation when he says: 'Any moment he's going to start getting bigger and bigger.' Compare the later despondency

in: 'Mr Kranky, for once, said nothing.' Taking the part of Mr Kranky, give the children the part of George. Together, read aloud the six lines of dialogue following 'about six feet long'. Ask: *Why does Mr Kranky emphasise 'think'? Is he becoming irritable?*

Marvellous Medicine Number Four

Comment on the brevity of this chapter. Discuss advantages and disadvantages of joining it to the last chapter. Does Dahl create more suspense with a separate chapter? Investigate the dialogue. Point out that Mr Kranky remains determined and optimistic. Ask: *How do you think George feels? How does Mrs Kranky differ from her husband?* (She is more realistic.) Ask the children to discuss question 4 on the Guided Reading bookmark.

Goodbye Grandma

Ask: *What does the opening line reveal about Mr Kranky?* (He will not give up.) Contrast this with Mrs Kranky's realistic 'Pack it in.' Comment that Grandma has been ignored for many chapters. Investigate her treatment now. Ask: *Why does Mr Kranky smile sweetly and encourage her to drink her 'tea'?* (He wants the medicine to harm her.) Comment that George and Mrs Kranky try to stop her. Contrast Mr and Mrs Kranky's attitudes, one enjoying Grandma's changes, and the other trying to save her. Ask: *How unpleasant is Mr Kranky?* Identify 'looking pleased', 'gleefully' and 'hooray'. Read the final speeches aloud. *Does Mrs Kranky's attitude change?* (She decides that Grandma's disappearance is 'all for the best, really.') Locate this extract near the end of the first chapter: 'A tingle of electricity flashed down the length of George's spine.' Link this to the book's final paragraph. Ask: *Has Dahl ended the story effectively? How?* Ask the children to discuss question 6 on the Guided Reading bookmark.

SCHOLASTIC
READ & RESPOND
Bringing the best books to life in the classroom

SCHOLASTIC
READ & RESPOND
Bringing the best books to life in the classroom

George's Marvellous Medicine by Roald Dahl

George's Marvellous Medicine by Roald Dahl

Focus on...
Meaning

1. Do you think Roald Dahl wants the reader to be pleased or horrified by George's decisions? Explain why you think this.

2. What predictions can you make about what may happen in the story from the title of this chapter?

3. How does George treat the medicine cupboard in a special way? Does this affect the atmosphere of the story?

4. Explain why the reader might find Mr Kranky a more interesting character than Mrs Kranky.

Focus on...
Organisation

5. Do you think the author uses dialogue effectively? Give an example and explain how it adds to the story.

6. What devices does the author use in to build up atmosphere and information about the characters?

Focus on...
Language and features

7. Identify four words in this section that you think are used effectively. Think of four words of similar meaning.

8. Why does the author divide the story into sections or chapters with headings? Is it an effective feature?

Focus on...
Purpose, viewpoints and effects

9. What point do you think the author is trying to make in this chapter? Explain why you say this.

10. Do you think Grandma is enjoying what is happening or is she feeling a different emotion? Give examples to support your opinion.

11. Is the author making a serious point here or is he just being light-hearted and funny? Give evidence for your answer.

12. Which character(s) does the author want you to sympathise with? Give examples of why you think that.

Extract 1

- Read this extract from the opening of the second chapter, 'The Marvellous Plan', where George thinks of an idea for strong action to deal with Grandma.

- Underline the words in italic font. Ask: *Why are they in italic font?* (for emphasis)

- Study the first paragraph. Ask: *Which verb shows George's frightened state?* (Circle 'was shaking'.) *Which verb reveals the extent of George's dislike of Grandma?* (circle 'hated') Underline 'witchy woman' and 'witchy smell'. Point out that Roald Dahl has already revealed that George fears Grandma may be a witch.

- Circle the question mark. Ask: *Is the reader being asked this question?* Suggest that George, in his thoughts, is questioning himself. In the subsequent three paragraphs, he suggests answers to himself.

- Underline the three uses of 'He would have liked to put'. Ask: *How long is each of these paragraphs?* (a single sentence) *Which word always separates its two clauses?* Circle the three uses of 'but'.

- Underline 'he didn't have' in the second part of the three paragraphs. Ask: *What effect does the repeated paragraph structure have on the reader?* (It emphasises George's struggle to find a plan.)

- Point out the long description of Grandma's medicine, dosage and effects as George tries to find an idea. Underline 'four times a day', 'didn't do her the slightest bit of good' and 'useless'. Point out that George has argued a case and reached a logical conclusion.

- Circle the exclamation marks in the final paragraph. Ask: *What mood do they suggest?* (George is happy and excited because he has an answer.)

Extract 2

- Read this extract is from the seventh chapter, 'Grandma Gets the Medicine', where George continues to dose Grandma with his medicine.

- Investigate the text in the first six paragraphs. Circle and comment on the numerous exclamation marks in Grandma's dialogue. Ask: *What do they imply?* (excitement and enjoyment) Suggest that these emotions are unusual for Grandma.

- Underline 'Dish it out!' and 'Just watch me go!'. Ask: *Is Grandma worried about hitting the ceiling?* (No, she wants to keep going up.) Compare Grandma's carefree mood with George's increasing caution. Underline evidence of this: 'That's the attic above you, Grandma!' and 'I'd keep out of there!'

- Suggest that the more medicine Grandma is given, the more daring she becomes. Underline: 'Give me another dose, my boy, and let's go through the roof!' Circle 'my boy' and two other examples of 'boy' used earlier by Grandma. Ask: *Does Grandma usually speak to George so pleasantly?* (no) *Do you think the new medicine has changed her for the better?*

- Examine paragraph seven. Circle 'shambles' and 'big hole' as Roald Dahl emphasises destruction. Underline from 'sticking up like a post' to 'head in the attic' and comment on the visual humour in this image of Grandma's ascent.

- Study the final paragraph. Ask: *What is George's mood now?* (He regrets giving Grandma so much medicine.) Comment on George's worry about his father's reaction. Ask: *Is Dahl beginning to describe a new character?* Circle 'He' in italic font twice. Ask: *What is being emphasised?* (George is responsible for this disaster.)

Extract 3

- Read this extract, taken from the final chapter, which brings the story, and Grandma, to an end.

- Circle 'grab' in the first paragraph. Suggest that the word conveys both the speed of Mrs Kranky's movement and the speed at which Grandma is disappearing. Ask: *Why is Mrs Kranky in such a hurry?*

- Identify and circle '*must*'. Ask: *Why has Roald Dahl used italic font? Is it necessary?* (It emphasises Mrs Kranky's protective feelings.) Ask: *Which verbs show the strength of Mrs Kranky's emotion?* Circle 'cried' and 'wailed'.

- Comment on Roald Dahl's effective comparisons when describing Grandma's size. Underline 'a matchstick', 'a pin' and 'a pumpkin seed'. Circle 'Then … Then …' Ask: *Why does Dahl stop completing his comparisons?* (There is nothing tiny enough.)

- Compare the two adults' attitudes after Grandma disappears. Ask: *Which word sums up Mr Kranky's reaction?* Underline 'Hooray'. In a different colour underline 'I've lost her!' and 'Mother, where are you? Where've you gone' Ask: *What is Mrs Kranky's emotion?* (distress)

- Read aloud Mrs Kranky's final dialogue. Ask: *What is surprising?* (her speedy acceptance of Grandma's fate) *Which words suggest it is partly a relief?* Underline 'She was a bit of a nuisance around the house.' How do the children react to these words? Are they meant to be humorous?

- Focus on George. Underline 'George didn't know what to think' and George didn't say a word'. Ask: *What does George think and feel about Grandma's disappearance?* (He is puzzled and he thinks magic is involved; he perhaps also feels a mixture of guilt and excitement.) Underline 'the edge of a magic world'.

Extract 4

- This extract, from a non-fiction book about alternative medicines, provides information about herbalism.

- Highlight the title. Explain that it indicates what the text is about.

- Underline and read aloud the opening statement. Ask: *What is its purpose?* (It introduces the subject.) Read aloud the next two sentences and discuss the first paragraph's function. Point out that having introduced the topic of herbalism, the paragraph then answers the questions What? Why? When?

- Question the children about divisions in the remaining text (paragraphs). Underline the bold words before paragraphs two to eight. Explain that such subheadings are common in information texts. Ask: *What is their purpose?* (They help the reader to find information they are looking for.)

- Circle 'cinchona', 'carotenoids', 'jujube', 'balsam poplar', 'birch', 'quassia' and 'St John's Wort' within the paragraphs. Emphasise that they are the correct names, essential in a text providing scientific information.

- Circle 'malaria'. Ask: *What is it?* (a serious fever caused by a mosquito bite) The correct term gives medical authenticity to the text.

- Read the fourth paragraph aloud. Refer to George's chant in the second chapter of the novel. Suggest that Roald Dahl is linking Grandma's irritability to this traditional herbal cure.

- Underline 'Even in modern times', in the first paragraph. Identify it as a fronted adverbial: a phrase functioning as an adverb and placed in front of the verb. Circle the comma after 'times'. Explain that a fronted adverbial is often followed by a comma.

Extract 1

The Marvellous Plan

George sat himself down at the table in the kitchen. He was shaking a little. Oh, how he hated Grandma! He really *hated* that horrid old witchy woman. And all of a sudden he had a tremendous urge to *do something* about her. Something *whopping*. Something *absolutely terrific*. A *real shocker*. A sort of explosion. He wanted to blow away the witchy smell that hung about her in the next room. He may have been only eight years old but he was a brave little boy. He was ready to take this old woman on.

'I'm not going to be frightened by *her*,' he said softly to himself. But he *was* frightened. And that's why he wanted suddenly to explode her away.

Well … not quite away. But he did want to shake the old woman up a bit.

Very well, then. What should it be, this whopping terrific exploding shocker for Grandma?

He would have liked to put a firework banger under her chair but he didn't have one.

He would have liked to put a long green snake down the back of her dress but he didn't have a long green snake.

He would have liked to put six big black rats in the room with her and lock the door but he didn't have six big black rats.

As George sat there, pondering this interesting problem, his eye fell upon the bottle of Grandma's brown medicine standing on the sideboard. Rotten stuff it seemed to be. Four times a day a large spoonful of it was shovelled into her mouth and it didn't do her the slightest bit of good. She was always just as horrid after she'd had it as she'd been before. The whole point of medicine, surely, was to make a person better. If it didn't do that, then it was quite useless.

So-ho! thought George suddenly. *Ah-ha! Ho-hum!* I know exactly what I'll do. I shall make her a *new* medicine, one that is so strong and so fierce and so fantastic that it will either cure her completely or blow off the top of her head.

Whopping
whopping

Extract 2

Grandma Gets the Medicine

'Come on, boy! Give me some more!' she yelled. 'Dish it out! I'm slowing down!'

George was still clutching the medicine bottle in one hand and the spoon in the other. Oh well, he thought, why not? He poured out a second dose and popped it into her mouth.

'*Owee!*' she screamed and up she went again. Her feet were still on the floor downstairs in the living-room but her head was moving quickly towards the ceiling of the bedroom.

'I'm on my way now, boy!' she called down to George. 'Just watch me go!'

'That's the attic above you, Grandma!' George called out. 'I'd keep out of there! It's full of bugs and bogles!'

Crash! The old girl's head went through the ceiling as though it were butter.

George stood in his bedroom gazing at the shambles. There was a big hole in the floor and another in the ceiling, and sticking up like a post between the two was the middle part of Grandma. Her legs were in the room below, her head in the attic.

'I'm still going!' came the old screechy voice from up above. 'Give me another dose, my boy, and let's go through the roof!'

'No, Grandma, no!' George called back. 'You're busting up the whole house!'

'To heck with the house!' she shouted. 'I want some fresh air! I haven't been outside for twenty years!'

'By golly, she *is* going through the roof!' George told himself. He ran downstairs. He rushed out of the back door and into the yard. It would be simply awful, he thought, if she bashed up the roof as well. His father would be furious. And he, George, would get the blame. *He* had made the medicine. *He* had given her too much. 'Don't come through the roof, Grandma,' he prayed. 'Please don't.'

Extract 3

Goodbye Grandma

When she was no bigger than a cigarette Mrs Kranky made a grab for her. She held her in her hand and she cried, 'How do I stop her getting smaller still?'

'You can't,' said Mr Kranky. 'She's had fifty times the right amount.'

'I *must* stop her!' Mrs Kranky wailed. 'I can hardly see her as it is!'

'Catch hold of each end and pull,' Mr Kranky said.

By then, Grandma was the size of a matchstick and still shrinking fast.

A moment later she was no bigger than a pin …

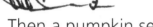

Then a pumpkin seed …

Then …

Then …

'Where is she?' cried Mrs Kranky. 'I've lost her!'

'Hooray,' said Mr Kranky.

'She's gone! She's disappeared completely!' cried Mrs Kranky.

'That's what happens to you if you're grumpy and bad-tempered,' said Mr Kranky. 'Great medicine of yours, George.'

George didn't know what to think.

For a few minutes, Mrs Kranky kept wandering around with a puzzled look on her face, saying, 'Mother, where are you? Where've you gone? Where've you got to? How can I find you?' But she calmed down quite quickly. And by lunchtime, she was saying, 'Ah well, I suppose it's all for the best, really. She was a bit of a nuisance around the house, wasn't she?'

'Yes,' Mr Kranky said. 'She most certainly was.'

George didn't say a word. He felt quite trembly. He knew something tremendous had taken place that morning. For a few brief moments he had touched with the very tips of his fingers the edge of a magic world.

Extract 4

Herbalism

Herbalism is the use of plants as medicine. Plants have been used in this way throughout human history. Even in modern times, herbalism is an alternative form of medicine that is still used by some.

The cinchona tree

The bark of the cinchona tree contains quinine. Quinine is widely prescribed by doctors to treat malaria. This drug is particularly popular in poorer countries that cannot afford to buy more expensive antimalarial drugs.

The balsam poplar tree

The balsam poplar grows in the north of North America. Its buds are covered with a sticky substance, used by herbalists in cough medicines. It has also been used as an ointment to aid the healing of wounds.

Carotenoids

Carotenoids are the plants that contain the colour pigment yellow, orange or red. People eating a diet that is rich in carotenoids from natural foods are likely to be much healthier. Example foods are pumpkins, sweetcorn and tomatoes.

The birch tree

The birch is native to northern and eastern North America. Folk medicine recommended chewing birch twigs for the relief of headaches and general pain.

The quassia tree

The quassia tree grows in southern and central American countries such as Mexico. Its wood contains a bitter substance that has been prescribed by herbalists to lower high temperatures.

The jujube tree

The jujube tree is widely cultivated in China. The tree's fruit is called a jujube. Jujubes are sometimes known as Chinese dates and they are used in traditional Chinese medicine for the treatment of stress, anxiety, irritability and insomnia.

St John's Wort

The majority of herbal medicines have not been scientifically tested. However, there have been many scientific studies to determine the power of St John's Wort. The results indicate that the herb can be effective in the treatment of mild depression.

GRAMMAR, PUNCTUATION & SPELLING

1. Adding prefixes

Objective

To add a prefix to a word to change its meaning.

What you need

Copies of *George's Marvellous Medicine*, printable page 'Prefixes'.

What to do

- Use this activity after reading the first chapter.

- Before the lesson, print and cut out the cards on printable page 'Adding prefixes'.

- Introduce the term 'prefix' – a group of letters added to the beginning of a word in order to turn it into another word.

- Write this on the whiteboard: 'Grandma showed George no <u>kindness</u>. She only showed him _____.' Suggest completing the second sentence by adding the prefix 'un' to the noun underlined. Write 'unkindness'. Ask: *What has happened to the meaning of the first noun?* (It now means the opposite.) Explain that not every prefix has this effect on a word.

- Give out the cards from the printable page 'Prefixes'. Make sure that everyone has one of each card. Explain that each word can become a new word by adding a prefix. Can the children match them?

- Share answers and write them on the whiteboard. Ask the children to list the new words and to write their meanings. Encourage them to use dictionaries.

Differentiation

Support: Let the children work with a partner and make greater use of dictionaries.
Extension: Challenge the children to make six new word cards to pair with the prefix cut-out cards. Or can they find any other words with prefixes in the first chapter of *George's Marvellous Medicine*, and use these instead? (disliking, disobedience, untidiness) Can a partner match them? What do the new words mean? What have they learned about the meaning of the prefixes?

2. Fronted adverbials

Objective

To use fronted adverbials.

What you need

Copies of *George's Marvellous Medicine*, interactive activity 'Adverbial hunt', printable page 'Fronted adverbials'.

What to do

- Complete this activity after reading the first chapter.

- Remind the children what an adverb is: a word adding meaning to the verb. Define 'adverbial': a phrase used instead of an adverb. Explain that an adverbial does not contain a verb.

- Display the interactive activity 'Adverbial hunt'. Let the children work in pairs, identifying each sentence's adverbial.

- Examine Screen 6 in the interactive activity. Comment that previous adverbials have followed the verbs. Ask: *What happens here?* (The adverbial precedes the verb.) Explain that an adverbial placed before the verb is a 'fronted adverbial'.

- Return to the other screens in the interactive activity. Then ask the pairs to move the adverbial, make it a fronted adverbial and then write their sentence on paper. Check answers together. As you read the new sentence aloud, the children should decide where a comma is needed. Ask: *What have you discovered?* (Fronted adverbials are usually separated from the remaining sentence by a comma.)

- Give out printable page 'Fronted adverbials' for the children to complete.

Differentiation

Support: Explain and complete a sentence on the printable page.
Extension: Ask children to identify three adverbs on the first two pages of the first chapter. Can they change them into fronted adverbials? Are punctuation changes needed?

3. Using conjunctions

Objective

To extend their range of sentences by using a variety of conjunctions.

What you need

Copies of *George's Marvellous Medicine*, photocopiable page 22 'Using conjunctions', interactive activity 'Making links'.

What to do

- Use this activity after reading the second chapter.

- Write on the whiteboard: 'Although George was a small boy, he had big ideas.' Identify it as a complex sentence: it has a main clause and a subordinate clause. What joins the clauses? Identify 'although' as a conjunction, a joining word or phrase.

- Point out George's mention of 'the ju-jube tree'. Display the interactive activity 'Making links' and read it aloud before working through a paragraph at a time with the children: ask the children to work in pairs to identify the conjunctions, giving answers to each other before you accept class answers.

- Ask: *What do you notice about the position of a conjunction?* (It may begin the connected sentence or be in the middle.)

- Give out copies of photocopiable page 22 'Using conjunctions'. Check that the children understand what to do. Encourage them to plan their answers before they write.

- Afterwards, let the children read their answers aloud, to themselves or to a partner. They will 'hear' where commas are needed. Share answers as a class. Point out the variety of conjunction links.

Differentiation

Support: Let partners work together. Encourage oral preparation of answers. Reduce the conjunction choice.
Extension: Ask the children to review a page of a recent story they have written, considering improvements: conjunction substitutions, position changes and short sentences that could join.

4. Spelling homophones

Objective

To spell and use homophones.

What you need

Copies of *George's Marvellous Medicine*, photocopiable page 23 'Spelling homophones', interactive activity 'Sorting homophones'.

What to do

- Complete this activity after finishing the book.

- Write this sentence on the whiteboard: 'Mrs Kranky knew that the new medicine was different.' Underline as shown. Let partners read the sentence to each other, listening carefully to the words underlined. What do they notice? (They sound the same.)

- Identify 'knew' and 'new' as homophones: they are pronounced in the same way. Can the children think of other homophones? Use 'sun/son', 'cereal/serial', 'currant/current' in oral sentences for the children to identify, define and spell.

- Display the interactive activity 'Sorting homophones' and explain that the words must be sorted into groups of homophones. Let partners share answers, before you ask volunteers to drag and drop words into place. As each set of homophones is created, ask half the class to read the words aloud. Do the listeners hear words that sound the same?

- Give out copies of photocopiable page 23 'Spelling homophones'. Explain that the children must fill the gaps with the correct words from the box of homophones. Encourage them to check the meanings of unfamiliar homophones.

Differentiation

Support: Put the children into pairs, and let an adult read the text and the homophones aloud before they write. Give support with unfamiliar homophones.
Extension: Challenge the children to think of 8–10 more pairs of homophones and use them correctly.

5. Marking speech

Objective
To punctuate sentences containing direct speech.

What you need
Copies *of George's Marvellous Medicine*, photocopiable page 23 'Marking speech', interactive activity 'Punctuating direct speech'.

What to do
- Do this activity after finishing the book.
- Introduce the term 'inverted commas'. Define these as marks that show speech within writing. They work in sets and mark the beginning and end of the words spoken by someone.
- Direct the children to appropriate pages in the last chapter. Can partners show each other a set of inverted commas? Ask them to identify the first and last words spoken?
- Ask: *What is strange about this book's inverted commas?* (This author uses single ones, not double.)
- Identify Mr Kranky's first speech at the beginning of the final chapter. Ask: *Which punctuation mark separates the sentence's spoken and unspoken words? Is it inside or outside the inverted commas?* Explain that a sentence's spoken and non-spoken words must be separated, usually by a comma, question mark or exclamation mark.
- Display the interactive activity 'Punctuating direct speech'. Invite children to choose the correct punctuation mark for each sentence. Point out that the choice of punctuation may be a matter of writer preference.
- Give out photocopiable page 23 'Marking speech'. Read the text aloud, emphasising spoken words, before the children punctuate it. Remind them to place the inverted commas in front of the first word spoken in a character's speech and after the last.

Differentiation
Support: Let the children hear the text more than once before placing inverted commas.
Extension: Ask the children to add some dialogue, being careful with punctuation.

6. Possessive apostrophes

Objective
To indicate possession by using the possessive apostrophe with plural nouns.

What you need
Copies of *George's Marvellous Medicine*, printable pages 'Possessive apostrophes' and 'Missing apostrophes'.

What to do
- This activity can be completed after reading the book, but with reference to the first chapter.
- Say this sentence aloud: 'She could know witches' secrets.' Explain that the sentence has two punctuation marks. Can the children make the marks on their individual whiteboards?
- Ask the children to hold up their whiteboards. They should have a full stop and an apostrophe. Ask which word needs the apostrophe and why? ('witches', in order to show ownership) Write the punctuated sentences on the whiteboard. Point out that you are placing the apostrophe after the 's'.
- Explain that the position of a possessive apostrophe is very important. Give out and read aloud printable page 'Possessive apostrophes'. Try applying the tip to your example sentence on the whiteboard.
- Give out individual copies of the printable page 'Missing apostrophes'. Ask the children to consider carefully where the apostrophe should be placed each time, before they mark it on the page. Remind them to check their list of rules and to apply the tip.

Differentiation
Support: Let children work in pairs, discussing their answers before placing the apostrophes.
Extension: Ask children to identify which rule has been applied each time. Can they identify six possessive apostrophes in a recent story they have written? Are they satisfied they have placed them correctly?

Using conjunctions

● Choose a conjunction to join each pair of sentences. Remember to use only one capital letter and one full stop in the new sentence.

so	since	but	where	although	so that	when	if
as	before	or	because	while	before	after	as

1. The bus reached the school. It stopped.

   _____

2. Josh wanted to stay with Mum. He was only five.

   _____

3. Josh was nervous. He tried to be brave.

   _____

4. Josh wriggled and squirmed. Mum combed his hair fiercely.

   _____

5. Josh's prized possession was a lucky badge. Dad had given it to him.

   _____

6. Mum pulled Josh by the hand. He went in the right direction.

   _____

7. A badge was worn in school. It was taken away.

   _____

8. Josh pressed his ear against the window. He heard no happy children.

   _____

   _____

Spelling homophones

- Use the words from the box of homophones at the bottom of the page to complete the children's conversation.

"Mum said that book's _____ scary for our age," said Emma. "I had bad dreams last _____ after reading it."

"_____!" said Matt. "Let's _____ what it's about!"

"Well, it's about an old lady who lives in a big, three _____ house. There are rumours that she could _____ a witch! Every day, some children walk _____ her house. One day she lies in _____ for them at a _____ near her _____. She waves her finger, and mutters strange words they don't _____. Straightaway it starts to _____ with _____! They are drenched! Then the _____ becomes thick and they can't _____ where _____ going. _____ that proves the rumours are _____!"

"_____ ," said Matt. "That's _____ good. When I _____ my parents about my last book like that, they said _____ am not _____ that sort anymore. They _____ give me silly ideas about my own _____ Grandma!"

to/two/too	knight/night	grate/great	here/hear
story/storey	be/bee	buy/by	wait/weight
plaice/place	gate/gait	no/know	pour/poor/pore
reign/rain	heir/air	see/sea	there/their/they're
sew/so	write/right	owe/oh	no/know
tolled/told	eye/I	allowed/aloud	might/mite
deer/dear			

Marking speech

- Jack and Emma are talking. Put inverted commas around the words they say and add the missing full stops, exclamation marks and question marks.

You must believe me shouted Jack.

No said Emma, gently.

Why can't I be right about witches asked Jack.

There's no truth in the stories explained Emma.

But you could take me to look at her begged Jack.

It would be rude said Emma.

I could pretend to be your assistant cried Jack.

You look too young said Emma.

You could disguise me shouted Jack.

No, I'm too sensible exclaimed Emma.

Then what can I do asked Jack.

Please go back to school and read a sensible book begged Emma.

PLOT, CHARACTER & SETTING

1. Finding answers

Objective

To predict what might happen from details stated and implied.

What you need

Copies of *George's Marvellous Medicine*, photocopiable page 29 'Finding answers'.

What to do

- Use this activity after reading the second chapter. When posing the questions suggested here, encourage partner discussion before progressing to whole-class exchanges.

- Help the children to scan the first two chapters. Draw attention to the small number of characters introduced. Ask: *Which character's name do you most notice?* Suggest that George may seem important because of the story's title. *Who do you think will be important in the rest of the book? Which item will matter?* (The medicine is in the book's title.)

- Ask the children to fill in the 'What I know about' section of photocopiable page 29 'Finding answers', summarising what they know so far about George, the medicine and Grandma.

- Suggest there are many questions unanswered. For example: will George carry out his plan? Ask the children to summarise the missing information.

- Invite the children to think about what may happen in the rest of the book and to write their prediction in the box at the bottom of the photocopiable sheet.

- Share predictions. Revisit them later, as you read the book, to see if any were right.

Differentiation

Support: Use partner discussion as a preparation for writing. Call attention to points to focus on.
Extension: Widen the study to include George's mother and father.

2. Using poetry

Objective

To prepare poems to read aloud and perform them.

What you need

Copies of *George's Marvellous Medicine*, printable pages 'Using poetry'.

What to do

- Complete this activity after reading the fifth chapter. When posing the questions below, encourage partner discussion before progressing to whole-class exchanges.

- Point out Roald Dahl's use of verse at the end of the chapter. Suggest the children scan the earlier chapters. Ask: *Does Roald Dahl use verse used on another occasion?* (yes, at the end of the second chapter) *What do the two poems have in common?* (rhyming couplets and spoken by George)

- Examine these two poems, or chants, by reading them aloud as the children follow. Ask: *What is the effect of the poems on you? Do they change the tone of the book?* (It becomes exciting and light-hearted.) *What character information do the poems supply?* (They show that George has an imaginative and creative brain.)

- Divide the class into four groups, assigning each group a different part of one of these chants, and distribute copies of the printable pages 'Using poetry' to each group as relevant. Allow preparation time, as the children examine their poem's words, agree how to perform it, allocate lines and rehearse.

- Let each group perform their poem, listeners being ready to decide how strongly the words affect their attitude to George and what he is planning and doing.

Differentiation

Support: Move among the groups, offering ideas and delivery assistance.
Extension: Ask the children to present a different section of a poem; or ask them to write their own poem that George might have composed, and to present this to the class.

PLOT, CHARACTER & SETTING

3. Changing moods

Objective

To draw inferences and justify them.

What you need

Copies of *George's Marvellous Medicine*.

What to do

- Complete this activity after reading the seventh chapter.

- Ask the children to re-read the book's opening page. What impression is given of the characters' feelings? Ask: *How does George feel?* (bored) Guide the children in scanning the rest of the first chapter. Ask: *Does George's mood change?* (boredom moves to terror) Invite the children to write two or three sentences describing the moods the writer creates and how he does this.

- Let the children scan the second chapter. Ask: *What are George's motives in making the new medicine?* Share ideas. Confirm that he wants to teach Grandma a lesson. Ask: *Could loneliness and boredom be factors? Does George remain frightened?* (He becomes very excited.) Ask the children to write two or three sentences describing the chapter's changing moods.

- Read aloud the first three paragraphs of the fourth chapter. Ask: *How does George feel?* Invite the children to look at the text. Is the author's choice of vocabulary revealing? Suggest that 'wheeze' (a joke) and '*those*' in italics convey excitement.

- Investigate together the seventh chapter. Ask: *How does the mood change?* Point out George's early excitement, but his worry, fear and regret at the end. Ask: *Do Grandma's feelings change?* Ask the children to write two or three sentences describing the changing feelings of Grandma and George during this chapter.

Differentiation

Support: Expect only one sentence each time and provide starting words.
Extension: Expect greater exploration of the text, supported by appropriate quotations.

4. Making an impression

Objective

To discuss words and phrases that capture the reader's interest and imagination.

What you need

Copies of *George's Marvellous Medicine*, photocopiable page 30 'Making an impression'.

What to do

- Complete this activity after finishing the book.

- Suggest that Roald Dahl often plays with language. Point out Grandma's yells, shouts, and screams of 'Oweeeee!' 'Whoopee!' and 'Oweee!' in the seventh chapter. Ask: *What is the effect of Roald Dahl's spelling of the exclamations in this way?* (Grandma's noises sound long and loud.)

- Comment on Dahl's expressive similes about Grandma in this chapter: 'like a jack-in-the-box' and 'dotty as a doughnut'. Ask: *What impact do Dahl's words have on your attitude to Grandma? Why?*

- Direct the children to the third chapter as George collects his medicine ingredients. Point out that Dahl puts the products' names and claims in capitals. George's thoughts and comments then relate these to Grandma: '…she was certainly a dirty old woman'.

- Indicate the animal names and illnesses in the fourth chapter. Ask: *How does Roald Dahl attract the reader's attention?* (He uses capital letters.) *How does he use the labels' words for humour?* (George's insults link them to Grandma, for example: 'grumpy old cow'; 'miserable old pig'.)

- Distribute photocopiable page 30 'Making an impression'. Encourage the children to re-read descriptions of the characters and their behaviour before they write about the effect of Dahl's words on them, quoting from or referring to the text.

Differentiation

Support: Encourage oral partner collaboration before writing.
Extension: Expect greater exploration of the text, supported by appropriate quotations.

5. Building humour

Objective

To identify themes and conventions in a wide range of books.

What you need

Copies of *George's Marvellous Medicine*, printable page 'Building humour'.

What to do

- Use this activity after finishing the book. When questioning, encourage partner discussion before whole-class exchanges.

- Ask: *Have you read any other Roald Dahl books?* Share information and then pick out these: *James and the Giant Peach, The Magic Finger* and *Matilda*. Explain that they all have a good (virtuous) child; a special power for the child (usually temporary); an unpleasant person (usually an adult).

- Guide the children to scan the first chapter of *George's Marvellous Medicine*. Point out George's virtues: politeness, helpfulness and patience. Give out printable page 'Building humour' for the children to write in the first box about George's character in the first chapter. Encourage textual references.

- Focus on Grandma in the first chapter. Point out her rudeness, demanding nature and nastiness. Ask the children to write about Grandma in the second box and to give evidence of her unpleasantness.

- Direct the children to the fifth chapter. Comment on the effect of the mixture's smell, the sparks George sees, his uncontrollable dancing and 'chanting strange words that came into his head out of nowhere'. Ask: *Is George gaining magic powers?* Read the book's final paragraph and ask: *Is magic implied here?* Let the children write in the third box of the printable page.

- Explain that these three parts of the story are a perfect, Dahl-style recipe for funny happenings. Ask the children to pick out three funny parts of the book and to write about them in the final box.

6. Exploring characters

Objective

To infer characters' feelings and motives from their actions.

What you need

Copies of *George's Marvellous Medicine*, photocopiable page 31 'Exploring characters'.

What to do

- Complete this activity after finishing the book.

- Comment that there are only four characters in this book. Ask: *Which one sticks in your mind? Is there a character you are not interested in? Why might this be?* Share views as a class.

- Let partners discuss how writers can reveal a character's personality (for example, through their actions, dialogue and comments from other characters). Create a class list of these.

- Suggest that the author often allows readers to form their own opinion, rather than telling them what to think. Refer the children to George's reaction to watching and smelling his first batch of medicine cooking: 'electric prickles ran along the backs of his legs' and 'he could have sworn he saw bright sparks flashing in the swirling foam'. The reader may infer that George is very imaginative and creative, or that he finds concocting a potion-like medicine very exciting.

- Give out photocopiable page 31 'Exploring characters'. Suggest that the children concentrate on one character at a time, working with a partner and searching the text to remind themselves of this person's characteristics. Encourage the children to choose their own adjectives for each character. Finally, ask them to write four new adjectives, one for each character.

Differentiation

Support: Ask them to choose just one adjective for each character.

Extension: Ask the children to write a paragraph describing one of the characters.

7. Following structures

Objective

To read books that are structured in different ways.

What you need

Copies of *George's Marvellous Medicine*, a novel written in first person (for example, *Hetty Feather* by Jacqueline Wilson), interactive activity 'What happens next?'.

What to do

- Complete this activity after finishing the book.

- Choose a novel written in the first person, such as, *Hetty Feather*. Read aloud from the opening pages. Comment on 'My', 'I' and 'me' and agree that the book is written in the first person.

- Let the children scan the early pages of *George's Marvellous Medicine*. Ask: *How does the author refer to George?* (he) *How does this book differ from the other novel?* (It is written in the third person.)

- Display the interactive activity 'What happens next?'. Put the children into pairs to discuss the events listed, find them in the book, and decide on their chronological story order. Ask the children to write their list. Share answers.

- Consider the Dahl's organisation of the book. How is it divided? (chapters of varying lengths) Do the children have other suggestions for its structure? Suggest that there could be chapters with time headings as the morning passes, or sections with the story told through different characters. Discuss how the story might be different if one of these structures had been used instead.

- What do the children think of the way the book has been structured, and the use of the third person?

Differentiation

Support: Help the children in finding the relevant chapter for each event.
Extension: Ask the children to name six other important events in the story for a partner to sequence. They should discuss why these events are important: what would the effect be if one of the events had not been included?

8. Asking questions

Objective

To ask questions to improve understanding of the text.

What you need

Copies of *George's Marvellous Medicine*, printable page 'Asking questions'.

What to do

- Use this activity after finishing the book.

- Suggest that the author often provokes questions in the reader's mind. Guide the children through scanning the eleventh chapter, 'Mr Kranky's Great Idea'. Ask: *What questions are in your mind by the end of the chapter?* Encourage partner discussion and share ideas. Write one example question on the whiteboard: 'What does Mrs Kranky think?'

- Give out copies of the printable page 'Asking questions' for the children to write their own questions.

- Scan the twelfth chapter with the children. Again, encourage partner discussion about questions they want answered by the chapter's end. Ask the children to write two questions. Repeat the scanning, thinking, talking and writing process for the remaining chapters of the book.

- Suggest that by the end of the book most questions should have been answered. Ask the children to write the answers, with quotations from the book, on their sheet. Are any questions unanswered?

- Let the children consider the whole book and unanswered questions provoked earlier, for example: 'Has Grandma's personality changed?'. Direct the children to the last part of the printable page to write two or three questions they still have. Ask: *How could Roald Dahl have answered these?* (He could have written a sequel.)

Differentiation

Support: Accept one question at each stage. Offer guidance with finding answers.
Extension: Expect more questions and specific location of answers.

Finding answers

● Fill in what you know and what you still have to learn. Then write what you think may happen in the future.

	What I know about...	What I don't know yet about...
George		
The medicine		
Grandma		

What I predict will happen

_____

_____

_____

_____

_____

Making an impression

● Complete the four boxes below.

Mr Killy Kranky
How do you react to these words? Why?

_____

_____

_____

How do you feel about the character? Why?

_____

_____

_____

'Whoopee!' she shouted. 'Hallelujah, here I come!'
How do you react to these words? Why?

_____

_____

How do you feel about the character? Why?

_____

_____

_____

'Here we go!' George cried out. 'Swallow it down!'
How do you react to these words? Why?

_____

_____

How do you feel about the character? Why?

_____

_____

_____

'Now you've done it' cried Mrs Kranky. 'You've cooked the old girl's goose!'
How do you react to these words? Why?

_____

_____

How do you feel about the character? Why?

_____

_____

_____

Exploring characters

● Draw lines to join two appropriate adjectives to each character. Then write one adjective of your own for each of the four characters.

protective

grumpy

greedy

creative

quiet

scary

optimistic

imaginative

caring

scheming

strict

puzzled

brave

clever

George

Your own adjective to describe

George: _____

Grandma

Your own adjective to describe

Grandma: _____

Mr Kranky

Your own adjective to describe

Mr Kranky: _____

Mrs Kranky

Your own adjective to describe

Mrs Kranky: _____

sensible

noisy

frightened

practical

excitable

bored

pessimistic

determined

frightening

loyal

unpleasant

lonely

nasty

selfish

▼ TALK ABOUT IT

1. Listen to your conscience

Objective
To use spoken language to develop understanding through speculating, hypothesising, imagining and exploring ideas.

What you need
Copies of *George's Marvellous Medicine*.

Cross-curricular link
Drama

What to do

- Complete this activity after reading the sixth chapter.

- Suggest that George is a mixture of good and bad characteristics: sometimes sensible, sometimes foolish. Point out, in the first chapter, his patient politeness with Grandma, and later, in the second chapter, his dangerous plan.

- Divide the class into two groups: Group A represents George's good side; Group B represents his bad side. Ask Group A to think of comments to persuade George to throw away his plan and to look after Grandma properly. Ask Group B to think of comments to encourage him to follow his plan and make new medicine.

- Organise the two groups into parallel lines facing each other. Take the role of George and walk down the 'alley' between the lines. As you reach each child, nod to them to speak their comments. At the end of the alley, make your decision.

- Choose some children to act as George, and repeat the conscience alley. Does each George reach the same decision?

- Try the activity with other situations from the book. Create smaller conscience alleys so that more children experience listening to their conscience.

Differentiation
Support: Let children speak with a partner in the conscience alley activity.
Extension: Ask children to plan a conscience alley situation for Grandma or Mrs Kranky.

2. In the hot seat

Objective
To take part in role play and infer characters' feelings, thoughts and motives.

What you need
Copies of *George's Marvellous Medicine*.

Cross-curricular link
Drama

What to do

- Use this activity after reading the ninth chapter.

- Suggest that the reader sometimes wants more detail about characters' feelings and motives than is given explicitly in the text. For example: why is Grandma so bad-tempered? Is Mrs Kranky worried about George looking after Grandma?

- Focus on George. Ask the children, after partner discussion, to agree on and write two questions they would like to ask him. Organise the children into groups of four to compare questions. Ask them to agree on two group questions.

- Explain the term 'hot seat': role play in which a character is interviewed. Put yourself in the hot seat as George. Turn away and try to make a change to your appearance. Turn and face the class, and invite the groups to ask you their questions, making sure that you answer in role.

- Let groups discuss what they found out about George's personality, feelings and motivation. Compare findings as a class.

- Select a different character: Grandma, Mr Kranky or Mrs Kranky. Repeat the task as a group activity, with one group member taking the hot seat to answer the others' questions.

Differentiation
Support: Provide the children with question starters.
Extension: Ask the children to make close references to the text.

3. What a story!

Objective

To give well-structured narratives for different purposes, including for expressing feelings.

What you need

Copies of *George's Marvellous Medicine*, photocopiable page 35 'What a story!'.

What to do

- Complete this activity after reading the tenth chapter.

- Point out that the chapter ends after an unusual day for everyone. Suggest that George, Grandma, Mr Kranky and Mrs Kranky will probably need to tell their story to someone.

- Guide the children through the main events, scanning from the beginning of the first chapter to the end of the tenth. Point out: the parents' absence; Grandma's taunts; George's fear; talk of magic; George's race against time; Grandma's reaction to the medicine; the damage to the house; Mrs Kranky's shock; Mr Kranky's hysterical exuberance; the use of a crane; Grandma's energy.

- Ask the children to decide which character to be: George, Grandma, Mr Kranky or Mrs Kranky. As storytellers, they must organise their facts in order, describe their feelings and include details, perhaps with information or memories known only to them.

- Give the children photocopiable page 35 'What a story!' and ask them to make notes and sketches to remind them what happened. Emphasise that they will be telling, not reading, their story. If appropriate, the boxes can be cut out of the photocopiable sheet and used as cue cards.

- Let the children practise their storytelling with a partner. Organise storytelling groups, so that everyone can experience speaking to a group.

Differentiation

Support: Suggest doing pictorial and one-word notes for a reduced number of cue cards.
Extension: Ask the children to take the role of an animal on the farm.

4. Stop or proceed?

Objective

To participate in discussions and debates.

What you need

Copies of *George's Marvellous Medicine*, photocopiable page 36 'Stop or proceed?', media resource 'Stop or proceed?'.

What to do

- Complete this activity after reading the eleventh chapter.

- Direct the children to where George says, 'I can't possibly remember all the hundreds of things'. Explain that you want the children to consider whether Mr Kranky should have given up his idea at this point or carried on.

- Put the children into pairs with a copy of photocopiable page 36 'Stop or proceed?'. Encourage partner and class discussion of the statements on the sheet. Point out that some statements may support either case, such as: 'Mr Kranky is a very excitable, enthusiastic person.'

- Ask partners to discuss and decide which side to support. (Ensure there are children supporting both sides.) The children must choose the statements to support their case. Suggest writing notes that list two or three new arguments; the children may like to consider the ethics of treating animals in this way, and the possible side effects of eating an animal that has been given such a concoction.

- Give yourself the role of chairing the debate and listening to arguments from both sides. Allow everyone to speak.

- Finally, sum up. Use media resource 'Stop or proceed?' and listen to the opinions. Do some children want to change their minds? Ask the children to make their final decision and vote.

Differentiation

Support: Children read out the statement that they think is the most effective argument.
Extension: Ask the children to argue a third way: persuading Mrs Kranky to work with them.

5. Changing the dialogue

Objective

To select and use appropriate registers for effective communication.

What you need

Copies of *George's Marvellous Medicine*, photocopiable page 37 'Changing the dialogue'.

What to do

- Use this activity after reading the twelfth chapter.

- Ask: *Is dialogue important to the story? Why?* (It can affect the mood, plot or characters.)

- Ask the children to re-read the dialogue between George and Grandma at the beginning of the seventh chapter, before she receives her first dose of medicine. Suggest that if Roald Dahl, when editing his story, had chosen to be kinder to Grandma, he would have changed the dialogue; and if he had done this, there would have been less reason for George to give her quite so much medicine.

- Put the children into pairs as George and Grandma. Ask them to improvise new dialogue so that George does not give the second dose to Grandma. Let the class listen to some pairs. Have they improved Grandma's character? How much have they changed the story?

- Repeat the exercise with the conversation between George and Mr Kranky in the early part of the twelfth chapter, before any medicine is given to a chicken. Encourage pairs to think about the effect they want from their new dialogue, such as: more humour, changed characters or changed plot. Let the class listen to and comment on the effect of some of the conversations.

- Give out photocopiable page 37 'Changing the dialogue'. Advise the children to decide the effect they want to achieve before they write.

Differentiation

Support: Let partners work together, speaking words before they write.
Extension: Ask the children to develop one of the conversations into a playscript for that scene.

6. Frozen moments

Objective

To use spoken language to develop understanding through speculating, hypothesising, imagining and exploring ideas.

What you need

Copies of *George's Marvellous Medicine*, printable page 'Frozen moments'.

What to do

- Use this activity after finishing the book. Explain the term 'freeze frame': the children create a still picture of a moment in the story.

- Guide the children in scanning the eighth chapter to the end of the book. Arrange the children in groups of four. Give each group one of the cards from the printable page 'Frozen moments'. Ask them to create a freeze frame for that part of the story. (Note that the last card only involves three children in the frame, as Grandma is too small to be seen.)

- Allow five to ten minutes for group discussion and rehearsal. Encourage every member of the group to contribute to decision making.

- Let each group present their freeze frame to the class. Can the class identify the story moment? Do they recognise the characters? Select individual characters to step out of the tableau and say what they are thinking.

- For other characters in the tableau, encourage the audience to consider what they seem to be thinking. Use 'thought tracking', when an audience member stands next to that character and speaks their thoughts aloud.

- Talk about the relevance of facial expression and body language in freeze frames. Ask the class: *Which expressions and body language helped you for thought tracking? How?*

Differentiation

Support: The teacher moves among the groups, offering suggestions for poses.
Extension: Ask the children to plan alternative freeze frames that will suggest different feelings.

What a story!

- Write notes to complete the cards below and use them to help you tell the story from the point of view of George, Grandma, Mr Kranky or Mrs Kranky.

✂----

Introducing yourself
Who are you?
How were you feeling first thing this morning?

Following a plan
Were you there when the ingredients were collected?
What happened in the kitchen?

Using the medicine
Were you in the house when the medicine was taken?
When did you know about the effects of the medicine?

Mrs Kranky arriving home
What were you doing?
What did you think was the most amazing thing that happened?

Tonight
What are you thinking and feeling now?

Stop or proceed?

● Read the statements below. Do you want Mr Kranky to give up his idea or to go on with it? Tick the statements which support your case.

I think Mr Kranky should:

☐ give up his idea.

☐ carry on with it.

Statements that support my opinion are:

☐ The family could become rich from selling George's medicine.

☐ George used a large number of ingredients.

☐ Mr Kranky is a very excitable, enthusiastic person.

☐ George is not used to seeing and talking to lots of people.

☐ Mrs Kranky is worried about the size of her mother.

☐ George's medicine, if successful, will make George famous.

● Think of your own statements to support your argument.

_____

_____

_____

_____

_____

Changing the dialogue

● Write new dialogue for these situations. Afterwards, say what effect your changes have on the story.

1. The bedroom scene

GEORGE: You're coming through my bedroom floor!

GRANDMA: _____

GEORGE: _____

GRANDMA: _____

GEORGE: _____

My changes have this effect: _____

_____

2. The kitchen episode

MR KRANKY: Now start making the medicine.

GEORGE: _____

MR KRANKY: _____

GEORGE: _____

MR KRANKY: _____

GEORGE: _____

MR KRANKY: _____

My changes have this effect: _____

_____

▼ GET WRITING

1. Magical chants

Objective

To discuss writing similar to that which they are planning to write in order to understand and learn from its structure, vocabulary and grammar.

What you need

Copies of *George's Marvellous Medicine*.

What to do

- Complete this activity after reading the seventh chapter. Encourage paired exchanges before whole-class discussion.

- Direct the children to George's chant at the end of the second chapter. Point out George's reference to 'magic' before he chants. Identify the chant at the end of the fifth chapter and its preceding paragraph. Ask: *What happens to George?* (A magic force seems to control his actions and words.)

- Read the fifth chapter's chant aloud. Invite discussion about its purpose and language. Ask: *Is the reader just being entertained? Does the chant emphasise unusual happenings?*

- Point out that George's chants are in a poetic form. Identify rhyme ('brew', 'blue'); sound repetition ('fume', 'spume'); alliteration ('spoondrift', 'spray'); and onomatopoeia ('fizzle', 'hissing'). Ask: *What is the rhyme pattern?* (rhyming couplets)

- Suggest that George could have chanted in the middle of the seventh chapter, perhaps after Grandma 'flipped herself clear out of the chair'. Explain that the children should write their own chant for this section. Encourage partners to discuss, share ideas and jot down words. They should write their draft chants alone, reading them aloud to each other afterwards for suggestions for improvement.

Differentiation

Support: Let partners collaborate on their writing. Or provide the opening lines of a chant for children to continue, such as: Jerky jolts and twisted turns/Fiery breath and fearsome burns.

Extension: Suggest children extend their chants, or write one for Grandma to say.

2. A point of view...

Objective

To choose pronouns appropriately for clarity and cohesion and to avoid repetition.

What you need

Copies of *George's Marvellous Medicine*.

What to do

- Use this activity after reading the seventh chapter.

- Let the children, in pairs, re-read the seventh chapter's first page and consider the author's writing style. Ask: *Which narrative form is used: third or first person?* (third person) *How can you tell?* ('He' and 'she' are used.) Explain that the author has written the book from the point of view of an outsider, telling the story of what happened.

- Scan the chapter together and discuss what happens when George gives Grandma his medicine. Investigate the medicine's early effects on Grandma and the initial reactions of the two characters: George is delighted and Grandma is horrified. Ask: *What is happening to Grandma by the end of the chapter? How are the two characters feeling?* (George is horrified and Grandma is delighted.)

- Suggest that it would be interesting if the reader could follow the story from the point of view of one of the two characters. Ask: *What pronouns would be used?* ('I' and 'me') Ask the children to become Grandma and write her account of what happened; this way the reader will focus on her feelings. Remind the children to be careful with pronouns.

Differentiation

Support: Reduce the rewriting to a shorter period of time or to Grandma receiving one dose of medicine.

Extension: Ask the children to describe the events from George's point of view and then compare the two narratives they have written.

3. Book review

To draft and write, organising paragraphs around a theme.

Copies of *George's Marvellous Medicine*, photocopiable page 41 'Book review', media resource 'Book reviews'.

What to do

- Use this activity after finishing the book.

- Ask the children to tell a partner what a book review is. Share ideas and ask: *What are reviews for? Who writes them? Where are they published? Who reads them?*

- Display example book reviews, such as those on interactive activity 'Book reviews'. Explain that there is no set format. Investigate common features: book title, author name and, if appropriate, illustrator details; story information (without revealing too much of the plot); personal like or dislike of parts of the book; a comment about its suitability for others.

- Hold a class discussion in which the children express their opinions of *George's Marvellous Medicine*. Emphasise that their views are not right or wrong: tastes are personal. However, encourage them to support their views with reference to the book. Ask: *What did you particularly enjoy about the book? Where, for you, was it most and least successful?*

- Give out photocopiable page 41 'Book review' for the children to draft a book review of *George's Marvellous Medicine*. Ask for whole sentences in most sections.

Support: Offer suggestions and encourage partner discussion when children are deciding what they most liked or disliked about *George's Marvellous Medicine*.
Extension: Let the children use their completed photocopiable as a plan to help them write a polished review for a magazine or website.

4. Changing the ending

To plan their writing by discussing and recording ideas.

Copies of *George's Marvellous Medicine*, photocopiable page 42 'Changing the ending'.

What to do

- Complete this activity after finishing the book.

- Help the children to scan the final chapter. Point out that these pages form the story's ending. Ask: *What is the function of a story's ending?* Compare ideas, agreeing on common features: (most) loose ends should be tied up; plot questions may be answered; the main plot problems ought to be resolved.

- Identify some of these features in the ending of *George's Marvellous Medicine*. Point out that the progress of George has been followed; his weekend boredom has been resolved; George's wish to do something about Grandma has been fulfilled; the problem of living with Grandma has been solved; questions about whether George could make a powerful medicine have been answered.

- Suggest that the author could have chosen to end the story differently. Let partners tell each other one possible change before you share some ideas as a class.

- Ask the children to write a new final chapter. Give out individual copies of photocopiable page 42 'Changing the ending' for them to plan their work.

- Let partners discuss their completed plans before, independently, writing their own ending.

- Invite some children to share their endings. Evaluate them as a class, to see if they share the common features of endings discussed earlier (problems resolved, loose ends tied up, and so on).

Support: Suggest the children create pictures of their ending before writing the text.
Extension: Ask the children to plan and talk about a second alternative ending.

5. Picture planning

Objective

To draft a narrative, creating settings, characters and plot.

What you need

Copies of *George's Marvellous Medicine*.

What to do

- Use this activity after finishing the book.

- Hold up two books: *Harry Potter and the Philosopher's Stone* and *Harry Potter and the Chamber of Secrets* by JK Rowling. Ask: What do the titles share? (the name 'Harry Potter') *Which one should you read first?* Explain that one book is the sequel to the other: it continues its story.

- Return to the ending of *George's Marvellous Medicine*. Point out that Roald Dahl has left the readers with many questions; not every loose end has been tied up. In particular, the reader wonders what will happen to Grandma.

- Invite partners to share ideas for a sequel. Ask: *What is the problem?* (Grandma has disappeared.) *How does George overcome it?* (He makes medicine.) *What helps him?* (He has magical powers.) *What is the ending?*

- Talk about a story's usual structure of four chronological sections: opening, something happens, events to sort it out, ending. Give each child a piece of paper to fold into quarters and number and label with these section headings ('Opening' and so on).

- Invite everyone to create a pictorial storyboard for their sequel. Each section may contain more than one picture and should show setting, character and plot.

Differentiation

Support: Let partners work together on the same story. Provide ideas for one or two sections.
Extension: Ask children to include interesting or powerful words related to plot, character and setting.

6. Building a story

Objective

To compose and rehearse sentences orally before writing a text.

What you need

Copies of *George's Marvellous Medicine*, interactive activity 'Building a story', photocopiable page 43 'Building a story'.

What to do

- Use this activity after finishing the book.

- Remind the children of the previous activity in which they planned a sequel to *George's Marvellous Medicine* as a pictorial storyboard.

- Present a pictorial storyboard that you have completed for another unrelated story. As a storyteller, recount what is happening in each picture.

- Explain that a story planner is useful when making notes. Display the interactive activity 'Building a story'. Demonstrate writing notes and point out that you are writing words and phrases, not sentences.

- Return to the children's pictorial storyboards from the previous activity. Suggest that they use their storyboard to tell their story to a partner.

- Give out individual copies of photocopiable page 43 'Building a story'. Ask the children to write notes for their sequel.

- Finally, ask them to write their story in one or more extended writing sessions. Encourage regular pauses to rehearse a sentence orally before writing it.

Differentiation

Support: Let children work with their partners from the 'Picture planning' activity, writing only one or two notes for each section.
Extension: Ask children to add two time conjunctions to each section's notes.

Book review

● Use this sheet to help you write a book review for *George's Marvellous Medicine*.

Title: _____

Author: _____

Illustrator: _____

About the story: _____

_____

_____

_____

My favourite part: _____

_____

My least favourite part: _____

_____

Who would enjoy this story? _____

_____

Now give the book a rating out of five by colouring the stars.

☆ ☆ ☆ ☆ ☆

Changing the ending

- Make notes to help you plan a new ending for *George's Marvellous Medicine*. Answer the questions about your own, new ending.

Does Grandma manage to snatch the cup of medicine from George? Does she just take just a small sip?
Is Grandma made completely invisible? Can her voice be heard?
Does Mrs Kranky keep feeling sad about her mother? Does Mr Kranky feel guilty?
Does the chicken with the long neck recover? What about the other animals?
Is George proud of his medicine? What is he thinking?
Does George feel his strange powers returning? Does he chant?

Other ideas I plan to include:

Building a story

- Use your pictorial storyboard to help you write planning notes for your story.

Opening	Something happens

Events to sort it out	Ending

ASSESSMENT

1. Assessing punctuation and grammar

Objective

To indicate possession by using the possessive apostrophe with plural nouns. To punctuate direct speech. To extend the range of sentences by using a variety of conjunctions.

What you need

Copies of *George's Marvellous Medicine*, printable pages 'Possessive apostrophes', 'Punctuation and grammar' and 'Punctuation and grammar (answers)'.

What to do

- Refer the children back to the book's opening paragraph and identify it as direct speech. Ask: *What punctuation is around the spoken words?* (inverted commas) *Why is there a comma after 'village'?* Explain that the comma separates the sentence's spoken and non-spoken words. Ask: *What other punctuations marks may do this?*

- Write this sentence on the whiteboard: 'Perhaps Grandma knew witches' secrets.' Circle the apostrophe. Ask: *What does it show?* (plural ownership by witches) Comment on the apostrophe's position after the 's'. Display a copy of the printable page 'Possessive apostrophes' and go over each rule.

- Direct the children to the book's sixth paragraph. Read it aloud and draw attention to 'while'. Ask: *What is the word's function?* Share information about other useful conjunctions: 'when', 'if', 'because' and 'although'. Create examples as a class.

- Give out individual copies of the printable page 'Punctuation and grammar' for the children to complete.

Differentiation

Support: Explain the tasks and reduce the quantity in each section of the assessment page.
Extension: Ask children to write their own sentences for the second and third sections of the assessment page.

2. Choosing words

Objective

To discuss words and phrases that capture the reader's interest and imagination.

What you need

Copies of *George's Marvellous Medicine*, dictionaries.

What to do

- Remind the children that Roald Dahl plays with language in this book, particularly when George feels magical power. The language is often chosen for its sound and the effect on the reader.

- Direct the children to the description of George's mixture as 'stuff', early in the fifth chapter, 'The Cook-up'. Point out the later use of 'whiff'. Ask: *Would you have chosen these words? What are more usual replacements? What does Roald Dahl achieve by his choices?* Share ideas, suggesting that 'mixture' and 'smell' are more usual alternatives. Dahl's choices are informal, childish language, encouraging the young reader to feel that the writer shares their, and George's, world.

- Re-read the long paragraph describing 'the marvellous mixture'. Ask: *What is the paragraph's effect on you? Which words help you to imagine both the scene and the future result on Grandma?* Share ideas.

- Identify unusual word combinations and write them on the whiteboard: 'spicy and staggering', fierce and frenzied', 'brutal and bewitching'. Put the children into pairs to look up the meanings using dictionaries. Ask: *Are the two meanings linked? What effect do the words have on the way you imagine the mixture? Is Roald Dahl using alliteration effectively?*

Differentiation

Support: Accept oral ideas and expect less writing.
Extension: Let children repeat the activity with vocabulary from the second chapter, 'The Marvellous Plan'.

3. Clear messages

Objective

To discuss writing similar to that which they are planning to write in order to understand and learn from its structure, vocabulary and grammar. To draft and write non-narrative material, using simple organisational devices.

What you need

Copies of *George's Marvellous Medicine*, interactive activity 'Clear instructions', photocopiable page 47 'Writing the recipe'.

What to do

- Help the children to scan the final five chapters. Ask: *How many times do George and Mr Kranky try to reproduce George's original medicine?* (three) *Why do they fail?* (George relies on memory.) Suggest that if George, when making his first medicine, had limited the ingredients, measured amounts and recorded it in writing, he could repeat it.

- Display interactive activity 'Clear instructions'. Ask: *Is the information laid out as clearly as possible?* (no, it is not) Let partners discuss ways for improvement. For each section of the interactive recipe, choose different pairs of children to offer suggestions. Do others agree.

- Investigate the recipe card's language and layout. Point out organisational devices: headings, separate lines and bullet points. Ask: *What verb form is used in the 'What to do' section?* Identify 'fry', 'add', 'spread', 'cover', 'place' as imperative verbs that give commands. Ask: *Where are they placed?* (They begin the sentences.)

- Ask the children to exchange ideas for a recipe for marvellous medicine with six to eight ingredients. Suggest the children make a rough draft before they write their recipe on photocopiable page 47 'Writing the recipe'.

Differentiation

Support: Encourage more partner collaboration in planning and offer support with spelling.
Extension: Ask the children to write a set of instructions for using their medicine.

4. Changing worlds

Objective

To identify themes in a wide range of books.

What you need

Copies of *George's Marvellous Medicine*, media resource 'Changing worlds'.

What to do

- Use this activity after finishing the book.

- Ask the children to re-read the book's final paragraph. Draw attention to the phrase 'a magic world'. Suggest that it is not magic that is important to George: it is changing his usual world that matters. Suggest that a desire for change is a major theme of this book.

- Direct the children to the second page of the book and George's thoughts: 'Looking after her all by himself was hardly the most exciting way to spend a Saturday morning.' Establish that George wants to change a boring Saturday.

- Point out that, during the story, three characters are excited about possible changes in their lives. Let partners share ideas about which characters they are. Share thoughts as a class.

- Display media resource 'Changing worlds'. Explain that at points in the story, each character shown on screen feels that life is going to change for the better for them. Read aloud the instruction on the screen. Put the children into pairs. As you show each picture, allow partner discussion, before you ask the children to write a paragraph independently about the special change that the character hopes for. Point out that the words below each picture may help.

Differentiation

Support: Accept simple explanations and more general reference to the text.
Extension: Expect a more detailed answer with closer reference to the text; ask children to identify this theme in other books they have read, and compare them.

▼ ASSESSMENT

5. Discussing books

To give well-structured narratives for different purposes, including for expressing feelings.

What you need

Copies of *George's Marvellous Medicine*, printable page 'Discussing books'.

What to do

- Carry out this activity after finishing the book.

- Explain that you will be reading *George's Marvellous Medicine* with next year's class, that you would like your new children to know a little about the story and that information from children in this year's class would be useful.

- Use partner and then class discussion to share comments, for example: some parts may make them laugh or feel sad; the main character is about their age; there are few characters.

- Explain that you want the children to speak about the book, but not simply read out what they write. Suggest that cue cards would remind them what to say next.

- Give the children printable page 'Discussing books' and ask them to make their cue cards. The content of each cue card should be brief and clear: notes or sketches to remind them what to say.

- After preparing their cue cards, let the children practise their speaking with a partner. Organise listening groups, so that everyone experiences speaking to a group.

- Arrange a visit from next year's class, so that the children can tell a visiting partner about the story.

Differentiation

Support: Allow partners to work together on their cue cards and oral retelling, each speaking for some of the time.
Extension: Expect children to speak at greater length and to provide interesting details.

6. Effective writing

Objective

To draft and write by creating settings and characters.

What you need

Copies of *George's Marvellous Medicine*.

What to do

- Carry out this activity after finishing the book.

- Direct the children to the book's opening page. Point out that Roald Dahl begins abruptly, without details of setting and characters. Ask: *How does the reader learn more?* Point out that facts are revealed gradually (Mrs Kranky's name is used in the ninth chapter), or the reader works them out (Mr Kranky is sometimes spiteful). Suggest that Dahl could have written an introductory chapter.

- Put the children into pairs to talk about the story's setting. Share information: the farm is isolated; it has a house, yard, outbuildings and numerous animals. Would the children add new details? Ask them to make brief notes. Repeat the process of partner and class discussion, and note making for the characters.

- Explain that the children are going to write the opening paragraphs of an introductory chapter. Let them work on a draft, composing sentences and reading them aloud to themselves and a partner. Encourage constructive feedback as partners help each other to monitor whether their writing makes sense. Ask them to write their polished paragraphs.

- Put the children into groups to read their writing aloud to one another. Remind them to consider their tone, intonation and volume so that their meaning is clear. Invite children to read their work to the class.

Differentiation

Support: Expect just one paragraph and let them read it aloud to you before they write.
Extension: Ask the children to write further paragraphs in their introductory chapter.

Writing the recipe

● Use the writing frame to create your own recipe.

How to make _____

Ingredients:

● _____

● _____

● _____

● _____

● _____

● _____

● _____

● _____

What to do:

_____

_____

_____

_____

_____

_____

_____

_____

_____

SCHOLASTIC

Available in this series:

978-1407-16066-5

978-1407-16053-5

978-1407-16054-2

978-1407-16055-9

978-1407-16056-6

978-1407-16057-3

978-1407-16058-0

978-1407-16059-7

978-1407-16060-3

978-1407-16061-0

978-1407-16062-7

978-1407-16063-4

978-1407-16064-1

978-1407-16065-8 JAN 2017

978-1407-16052-8 JAN 2017

978-1407-16067-2 JAN 2017

978-1407-16068-9 JAN 2017

978-1407-16069-6 JAN 2017

978-1407-16070-2 JAN 2017

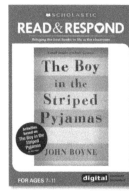
978-1407-16071-9 JAN 2017

To find out more, call: 0845 6039091
or visit our website www.scholastic.co.uk/readandrespond